T0209441

DAILY
Elemental Messages

A YEAR LONG JOURNEY WITH
THE ELEMENTAL REALM

ANNE LAFRANCE

BALBOA.
PRESS

A DIVISION OF HAY HOUSE

Copyright © 2019 Anne Lafrance.

Interior Graphics/Art Credit: Anne Lafrance

All rights reserved. No part of this book may be used or reproduced by
any means, graphic, electronic, or mechanical, including photocopying,
recording, taping or by any information storage retrieval system
without the written permission of the author except in the case of
brief quotations embodied in critical articles and reviews.

This book is a work of non-fiction. Unless otherwise noted, the author
and the publisher make no explicit guarantees as to the accuracy of
the information contained in this book and in some cases, names of
people and places have been altered to protect their privacy.

Balboa Press books may be ordered through booksellers or by contacting:

Balboa Press
A Division of Hay House
1663 Liberty Drive
Bloomington, IN 47403
www.balboapress.com
1 (877) 407-4847

Because of the dynamic nature of the Internet, any web addresses or
links contained in this book may have changed since publication and
may no longer be valid. The views expressed in this work are solely those
of the author and do not necessarily reflect the views of the publisher,
and the publisher hereby disclaims any responsibility for them.

The author of this book does not dispense medical advice or prescribe the use
of any technique as a form of treatment for physical, emotional, or medical
problems without the advice of a physician, either directly or indirectly. The
intent of the author is only to offer information of a general nature to help
you in your quest for emotional and spiritual well-being. In the event you use
any of the information in this book for yourself, which is your constitutional
right, the author and the publisher assume no responsibility for your actions.

Any people depicted in stock imagery provided by Getty Images are
models, and such images are being used for illustrative purposes only.
Certain stock imagery © Getty Images.

Print information available on the last page.

ISBN: 978-1-9822-1877-5 (sc)
ISBN: 978-1-9822-1878-2 (e)

Balboa Press rev. date: 12/26/2018

Dedication

I dedicate this book to all the beings in the Elemental Realm who believe in me, my existence and trust in me.

Acknowledgement

Brother Gnome and Fairy Salunda who have been my guides in the beginning of my journey into the Elemental Realm.

Jeana Koch, my soul sister who supported me.

My daughter and my cat who sacrificed mother time, so I can write the book.

Introduction

The Elemental Realm is full of beings from nature that reside in the higher vibrational dimensions. There are of course the elemental beings we commonly know as the elements, fairies, gnomes, elves, leprechauns, goblins, trolls, devas, wizards, princesses, princes, queens, kings and so many more. There are also the nature spirits in trees, plants, rocks, crystals and animals.

Then there are the higher dimensional beings, which includes mermaids, dragons, unicorns, personal guides, goddesses, gods and archangels, all of which play a role in the Elemental realm. This Realm is so vast that I could not possible list them all. They are all directed by Gaia, our Mother Earth, and Source, the spirit that resides in us all and in everything, the oneness.

A word on the 4 elements

These are the basis from which everything is created and works from. They have a collective and an individual consciousness. I relate to them in the following way:

- Air element being: sylphs
- Water element being: sprites
- Fire element being: sparks
- Earth element being: terra

A word on the Nature Gods & Goddesses

Many gods and goddesses work with nature. I have included the main ones who work with the Elemental Realm begins. Here is a brief summary of each of them.

- Maeve is a Celtic fairy queen goddess who oversees the elemental realm and their magic.
- Damara is a Celtic goddess and fairy princess that protects and guides children and elementals.
- Aine, pronounced Awnia, is a fairy queen goddess who guards animals and crops.
- Pan is a nature god who prefers mountains and woodland areas.
- Cerunos (also known as Cernunnos) is Celtic horned god of forests and animals. He often appears as a white stag but can appear as anything. He is the full cycle of nature, helps usher in life, supports growth, and when it is time, he guides the life through the transition, back to the beginning as well as overseeing the bodily decay.
- Green Man is the essence of vegetation. He runs his beingness, his energy through vegetation to fuel and help clear any stagnation.

A word on Other Beings

Many other beings work with this realm even though they are part of another realm. Here are but a few who wished to be part of this book.

- Archangel Ariel is the one who works primarily with nature.
- St. Francis of Assisi is a saint known for his connection to animals and especially birds.
- Green Tara is an ascended master who works with the Elemental Realm beings and the green ray.
- Phoenix is a fire bird of transmutation and rebirth.
- Gaia: The nature being who is Mother Earth. She oversees all in the Elemental Realm and directs all activities for the greatest and highest good of all. She works relentlessly to bring everything into balance and maintain it. She is currently going through many great shifts in order to ascend to higher dimensions. She is the true super mom!

The Elemental Realm beings are showing themselves more and more so that we can work with them and with nature. The Nature beings communicate with us all the time. They leave signs everywhere. Go outside, the nature beings will meet you there. The elementals watch and observe you to see what your true intentions are. They can look through all sorts of eyes. Messages come in all forms.

I have learned so much in working with the Elemental Realm, particularly in putting this book together. I am so grateful to beings in the Elemental Realm for their wisdom and humbled to be a bridge between the Elemental and Humanity Realms.

How to Use this Book

This book contains messages from the various beings of the Elemental Realm. Many beings from the Elemental Realm have come forth as anonymous representation of their species yet there are a few specific individuals from the area in which I live in who wanted to be part of this book in order to share their wisdom. There is a message for everyday. Some are simple, and others delve deeper with the wisdom, yet all are equally powerful.

The book loosely follows the natural rhythm of the year but is laid out so that you can begin your journey on any day of the year. If you would like a pertinent message from your team for that day, you can flip to any page to gain a message.

Day 1

Fairy:
Take time to have fun and enjoy life!

Day 2

Pan:
Nature is always smiling, are you noticing?

Day 3

Gnome:
Your energy expands out with feelers. Notice if
they are sourcing nutrients or draining energy.

Day 4

Sprite:
When the energy flows through you,
you have to flow with it.

Day 5

Tree Spirit:
Trees often display hearts to remind people to
love themselves. Love yourself. Share the love.

Day 6

Goblin:
There will always be shadows. They are everywhere. It
is important to investigate your own shadows. Accept
the possibility that there are treasures laying there.

Day 7

Leprechaun:
Welcome to the Elemental Realm. It is my
most sincere hope that you invite us in to guide
and help you so that you may continue this
journey with us with an expanded heart.

Day 8

Fairy:
Creativity is the willingness to play with
what is in your presence in the moment.

Day 9

Dragon:
Know your power.

Day 10

Mermaid:
No matter the depths you find yourself in, you can
call in the light and then you can swim towards it.

Day 11

Gnome:
Don't let the pricklies get you down.

Day 12

Spark:
Tune into your inner beauty and light it up.

Day 13

Fairy:
Flowing joy through you will fill you with sparkles.

Day 14

Rock Being:
Time to slow down and go within.

Day 15

Mermaid:
With all of your love, place your attention
towards the vibrations you send out. More
importantly notice what comes back.

Day 16

Tree Spirit:
Beauty is revealed through the undressing of letting go.

Day 17

Wizard:
It is time to gather your treasures, gifts,
tools and supplies for all of the alchemy
you will perform during the winter.

Day 18

Gnome:
Get outside and connect to nature

Day 19

Dragon:
It is time to know the truth; your truth & the universal truth. Go within and listen.

Day 20

Unicorn:
Magic is everywhere.

Day 21

Green Man:
I am ever present like the leaves that I appear in. I am always sharing information. I ask the fairies, elves and all the elementals to move branches and leaves to show images. Pay attention to these. They are meant for you to see. Open your heart and imagination to access the truth. If you see a bunny, you see a bunny? What does it mean to you. If you see something scary, what are you afraid to look at within yourself? It is always a message specific to you. You will see what you need

to see. Someone else could see something completely different because their perspective is different. Their path and needs are different. There messages are reflections of our truth and are ever present as the leaves come and go and come back for a new season you too grow and evolve, and your message needs will change.

Day 22

Sylph:
The full moon lights your way. The new moon leaves darkness. Whether your path is lit or not, call on us and the Moon Goddess to help guide your way.

Day 23

Damara:
Fill your being with compassion and show kindness for all beings.

Day 24

Deva:
Your blueprint has all the instructions for your beingness. It does not mean that you are powerless to those blueprints. You are the architect. Feel free to redesign the plans at any time.

Day 25

Ice Elf:
Feel into the magic of the frost. It is a protective layer but who says you can't have fun with it! The ice crystals dance and shimmer in the sun. Enjoy it.

Day 26

Troll:
Often the mind wanders and gets lost in the unconscious thoughts and emotions. Should you find yourself in a situation where you need to focus, such as driving, call on me to help you direct your thoughts and emotions to the task.

Day 27

Fairy:
Be the King or Queen of your mountain.

Day 28

Dragon:
Go find your inner child and play a little. Invite me over and I can teach you the lighter side of being a dragon.

Day 29

Green Man:
Elementals love to use the elements in
nature to reveal themselves.

Day 30

Sylph:
Everywhere there is an opportunity for
change, which always leads to rebirth.

Day 31

Unicorn:
Love yourself. Allow love to flow in and through
you. You are the only one keeping it out. I can
help you. Understanding what love truly is and
brining you into it is a unicorn specialty.

Day 32

Fairy:
Remember to have fun in all that you do!

Day 33

Leprechaun:
The elementals like to have fun and
show up in various ways.

Day 34

Terra:
I cycle the organic matter from creation to
growth to decay. Set the intention how you want
your body to cycle through this process.

Day 35

Frost Elf:
We communicate with you via images in the
frost. We are overjoyed when you stop to admire
our work and take a moment to see what
messages we have left. If you do not understand
them, know that we can work on that.

Day 36

Goblin:
When you work you unearth your
unconscious baggage, I sparkle.

Day 37

Gaia:
I provide all of the resources that you require as a living being. Know that I can support you in many more ways if you take time to connect with me.

Day 38

Gnome:
We are amazing teachers. Seek our counsels on how best to grow anything in your life. We can be serious, but we have a playful side too.

Day 39

Troll:
If your obstacles feel unsurmountable, call
on me. I can easily move boulders.

Day 40

Green Tara:
Love really does conquer all. It starts with
knowing how to love yourself.

Day 41

Unicorn:
Believe in the elementals. We believe in you!

Day 42

Tree Spirit:
You can stand strong in the face of adversity
when you are securely grounded.

Day 43

Fairy:
Span your wings, explore the colours
and take in the beauty.

Day 44

Gnome:
Nature is love. Nature is always sending us love. Take a moment to send love to nature but more importantly love nature. ♥

Day 45

Leprechaun:
Laugh with life and you will learn a lot while enjoying life.

Day 46

Elf:
Managing your boundaries ensures that your heart can remain open.

Day 47

Unicorn:
I would like to know: What is your unique power?

Day 48

Dragon:
We are ready to serve when you are ready to ask.

Day 49

Aine:
When you flow through life consciously aware and take responsibility for your issues then your animal companions are free to be fully loving and enjoyable companions.

Day 50

Mermaid:
Go exploring, there are treasures everywhere; even in the darkest scariest corners!

Day 51

Snow Fairy:
We align the snow crystals, so the sun can reflect in them and make them sparkle. We do this to remind you to do the same in your life.

Day 52

Spark:
We are always available to help transform energies. Just light a candle and ask.

Day 53

Leprechaun:
Be brave enough to express joy and to act silly. Step
away from societal constrictions and into authenticity.

Day 54

Unicorn:
Trust

Day 55

Rock Being:
We love watching you walking by in nature.
It amuses us when you are unconscious, but
we are overjoyed when you are present in the
moment and enjoying your surroundings.

Day 56

Gnome:
There is as much life underground as above. You just
need to know how to look. We can show you how to
dig deep within to understand your underground life.

Day 57

Elf:
Running is good for the body. Running away is only delaying the inevitable. Running in joy and celebration means living in the moment even if it means running towards your challenge.

Day 58

Dragon:
Call on me for protection at any time for any reason. I will be there in an instant.

Day 59

Archangel Ariel:
I can help you in any efforts in working with nature, the nature beings and elementals

Day 60

Snow Fairy:
Enjoy the snow. Each flake holds the vibrations it comes in contact with and when it melts that vibration spreads. What vibrations do you want to feel in the spring?

Day 61

Deva:
When you are ready, I can help you
reprogram your blueprint and templates.
You will know when the time is right.

Day 62

Terra:
You are of the earth. You are made of organic
material. You are one with all of the beings
on this planet. You are one with Gaia. Align
your heartbeat with Gaia's heartbeat.

Day 63

Unicorn:
The wisdom is inside but you reach
it via the imagination.

Day 64

Pan:
Connect with a tree or another plant today. Each
one has a spirit waiting for you to reach out to.

Day 65

Water Dragon:
Get in the flow, go with the flow

Day 66

Fairy:
Flashing your true colours or blending into the
background; what is the moment calling you to do?

Day 67

Dragon:
Do not fear us. We look fearsome only to get your
attention, so you can look at the lies you tell yourselves.

Day 68

Goblin:
I work with the many beings involved in decaying
matter. This is a natural process that occurs
regardless of any resistance. When it comes to your
personal being, knowing what you are decaying
and what is flourishing is the key. I can show you
how to use the decay to feed what is flourishing.
You must choose which will be which.

Day 69

Rock Being:
We inhabit all rocks from the tiniest grain of sand
all the way up to the highest mountain. We are
on the ground, underground, below the water and
up above you. You can access from anywhere. We
hold and share qualities unique to our status and
environment but also the great consciousness. We
are happy to share any wisdom that you seek.

Day 70

Fairy:
Dream your heart's desire.

Day 71

Mermaid:
I can guide you through troubled waters
and challenging weather. Just ask me
and I am there by your side.

Day 72

Wizard:
Nature is abundant. Be ready to receive with open arms!

Day 73

Green Tara:
If you are looking to work with the beings of the Elemental Realm ask me to help guide you. We can cast the net wide or focus in to gain a specific truth.

Day 74

Deva:
Fear not the fog. When you come across fog, it is a signal to slow down and go within. Your vision may be limited but if you take a moment you will notice that you can feel into it with much more ease. Trust that you can guide yourself to clarity.

Day 75

Ice Elf:
Don't be afraid of the cold. Call on us and we can direct the freezing away.

Day 76

Fairy Queen Maeve:
Our work is serious, but it doesn't mean that we must be serious or miserable. We approach life with love, joy and play. This energy fuels us and we extend it into all our tasks.

Day 77

Imp:
Transformation can happen regardless of the surroundings. It happens within and when you do, you brighten the surroundings.

Day 78

Tree Spirit:
I see you & your beauty; do you?

Day 79

Fairy:
Be brave and explore all your feelings as they
are clues that guide you to the treasure.

Day 80

Leprechaun:
Remember that you are always touched
by a rainbow when the sun shines.

Day 81

Deva:
We are all going through metamorphosis and all
at different stages of the process. It takes time
to go from caterpillar to butterfly ready to take
flight. Be gentle with yourself. Sending love.

Day 82

Fairy:
What are you allowing to eat up your beauty?

Day 83

Earth Dragon:
Remember to ground and to become part of the land.

Day 84

Gaia:
You are a precious being. You are a magnificent
child of the Divine therefore I welcome you
here and love you as my own. There is nothing
that you can do that can change that.

Day 85

Cerunos:
The fairies enjoy play and love it when humans play.

Day 86

Elf:
Sometimes standing back and being
quiet is the best approach.

Day 87

Spark:
When the sun shines on you, know that it is I who
kisses your skin to give you the nutrients you need
to transmute debris in your body and to support
it. Acknowledgement can facilitate the process.

Day 88

Deva:
Purging is a natural process of the body to
release what is no longer needed. If you resist
and worry about it, you will suppress it. This will
result in the amplification of its effects later.

Day 89

St. Francis:
Many have unconditional love for animals yet not
for themselves. One cannot truly be in a space of
unconditional love if there is non for the self.

Day 90

Fairy:
Fungus has a purpose, to transform the material around it. It is a slow process because time is an illusion. What are you transforming in and around you? Are you allowing enough time for it?

Day 91

Imp:
Rather than swatting away what irritates your face it and talk to it. Find out what it wants and give it. You will find life much more peaceful if you do.

Day 92

Tree Spirit:
We all send roots out to connect with others. Are you doing so consciously or unconsciously? What is being exposed in your life?

Day 93

Sprite:
The possibilities are limited only by your imagination.

Day 94

Wizard:
I can help you move out of the mind and into the heart. There we can alchemize lead into gold.

Day 95

Fairy:
In the rebirth and renewal set clear intentions for going forward.

Day 96

Dragon:
Do not be afraid to be curious. Trust that you are protected when you ask. Investigate, play, connect.

Day 97

Wizard:
When learning to work with the higher dimensions, this is my advice. Practice, practice, practice. One or two attempts does not equal mastery. It takes time, it takes work, it takes belief and trust, but I know that you can do it.

Day 98

Spark:
Embrace the fire element within you and call on us
or any fire being to assist with transmutations!

Day 99

Gaia:
I am a living breathing being like you. Take care of me
and I can continue to ensure you are provided for.

Day 100

Fairy:
Look past what appears to be an end of blooms to
see what new buds are coming up in your life.

Day 101

Snow Fairy:
Sometimes you need to just step back and
let the winter beings do their work.

Day 102

Tree Spirit:
Look beyond limitations.

Day 103

Fairy Queen Maeve:
The elementals will play with the shadows to show images. The elementals used the negative space to bring images through in this picture. What images do you see? What do they mean to you?

Day 104

Sylph:
Love on the wings of an angel is forever yours.

Day 105

Wizard:
You cast spells with your words. These spells bind, lock and block your progress. Cast wisely!

Day 106

Tree Spirit:
When you are creating the fruit you bear, note
that the potency depends on what occurred
long before they appear on the branches.

Day 107

Fairy Jumpfly:
Uplift your office space with beautiful items that
make you feel wonderful and plants that detoxify
the air. Get to know the fairy that is in charge of
the plant and build a brilliant relationship. This
fairy can help you amp your energy when you are
feeling down or overloaded with external stimuli.

Day 108

Spark:
Celebrate your anger! Know that when you bubble
with heat, that it is a moment of great opportunity
to transmute something into an amazing higher
vibration. Look into the flames within. Hear it sizzle
and crack. It is telling you what is wrong in the
moment. What it is telling you? Now use it to burn it
away. Watch the fire build stronger. Funnel this strong
flame to heart and use it to fuel heart based action.

Day 109

St. Francis:
Show as much compassion for the creatures viewed as less pretty such as the insects and mollusk as you do the fluffy animals. These creatures mirror aspects of yourself that need to be looked at and loved.

Day 110

Fairy:
Dive face in.

Day 111

Leprechaun:
Follow the rainbow to your true treasure.

Day 112

Rock Being:
When you come upon the stillness in nature, that is
a reminder to be still within. Stop and notice what
your body is doing, what your mind is saying, what
your emotions are up to. Yes, those mosquitos, those
deer flies, those black flies, they are the unconscious
thoughts that don't allow you to enjoy the stillness.
Practice and soon you will notice in nature, no flies.

Day 113

Elf:
I can help you find your inner song. As I sing
to the plants, you can sing your song and our
joined melody can flutter through the fields.

Day 114

Archangel Ariel:
I can help you in any efforts in working with
nature, the nature beings and elementals.

Day 115

Tree Spirit:
All plants are masters at transmutation. We circulate the toxins up and down our membranes and convert what we can to beneficial elements. Your body can do the same if you allow it to. Even though our bodies may be different, we can show you how to be efficient transmutaters like us.

Day 116

Snow Fairy:
When the snow melts it indicates transformation is about.

Day 117

Damara:
Be as gentle with yourself as you would a baby.

Day 118

Sylph & Terra:
Call on us to bring your attention into focus and ground that into your body to keep from wondering.

Day 119

Troll:
When you are feeling down, frustrated, worried, afraid or angry, call on me and I will walk beside you. When you are ready, I will help you to shake those vibrations loose, so you can clear them.

Day 120

Phoenix:
Let go of fear. It is a control mechanism to keep you paralyzed in the lower vibrations, so you do not expand to greater heights. Fear is an illusion for you cannot control anything. Fear feeds fear. Let trust be the fuel to flame your fire. Use it to soar to the greater heights where your true essence lies.

Day 121

Wizard:
When you believe that is when the magic opens.

Day 122

Tree Spirit:
There is no need to do it all alone. We lean on each other, entwine our branches and reach out with our roots to lend a hand. Partnering up is rewarding.

Day 123

Fairy Queen Maeve:
Your web will catch more than food.
What are you collecting?

Day 124

Winter Fairies:
When it is time to go within we protect and blanket nature with frost, snow and ice. The frost sends a signal to all of nature that it is time for this process to begin. The snow promotes stillness and sleeping. The ice provides protection. There is ebb and flow through the winter to promote various cycles of the dreaming process. We encourage you to look at your dreaming process and cycles. Are you using the natural shutting down and protective mechanisms to avoid something or to go within? Do you flow with the cycles? Do you wake and cultivate the dreams, or do you keep yourself busy trying to clear the snow

and hack at the ice? Winter is a necessary part of the yearly cycle. We encourage you to embrace it.

Day 125

Unicorn:
I am always available for assistance. Do you ask?

Day 126

Fairy:
Call on us to help you with your gardens or planted greenery. We can guide you on how best to plant, care for and manage them.

Day 127

Leprechaun:
We happily play the trickster but know that it is for your own good. It serves to pull you out of the groove you got stuck in. It is like a slap in the face to wake you up; without harming you. We do this because we love you.

Day 128

Gnome:
Digging for the treasures within
is easier than you think.

Day 129

Fairy:
Sometimes we say hello to you by wafting the air with
plant fragrances. If you notice them, wave back.

Day 130

Elf:
Camouflage. Are you able to make your
self seen in your environment?

Day 131

Green Tara:
When the temperature drops and the wind gusts, it is
time to go within to draw on your inner resources.

Day 132

Troll:
The tunnel holds more than just the light at the end.
It has texture, crevices, smooth and rough areas.
Make sure to capture the gifts along the way.

Day 133

Wizard:
Call on me to help you clear the spell of perfection
and accept the gifts in the blemishes.

Day 134

Aine:
Setting clear boundaries is healthy and necessary.
Your animal companion understands this. It is
important to apply this in all areas of your life.

Day 135

Dragon:
Ask us to transmute the old, even if
you are just sweating it out.

Day 136

Tree Spirit:
Are you aware of your surroundings? Are
you aware of your internal environment? Pay
attention; notice what is in and around you.

Day 137

Pan:
Energies in life are superimposed; you fit in the layering.

Day 138

Fairy:
When you are out in nature, notice the placement of
the rocks. We strategically placed rocks in a certain
way and imbued them with a special energy message.
Connect to the placement and see what comes to you!

Day 139

Sprite:
Do not be fooled by above appearances. Yes, there is
beauty but the roots plunge deep and that is where
the true magic is. It is the journey from the roots to
above the water level where the strength of being lies.

Day 140

Fairy:
Sometimes you just need to shine your
light through the shadows.

Day 141

Unicorn:
When you feel like you are in an unsafe
place, call upon us to keep you safe. Ask us to
clear the fear that attracts scary events.

Day 142

Damara:
Sometimes an elemental being will get lost. Whether it
is a young one who is not completely ready to step out
or whether it is because they get confused in the human
interference, they can use our help. Should you notice
a lost elemental, call me and I will assist them home.

Day 143

Gnome:
Ground. Take your skills and ground them into reality
for the tribe and transmute what no longer serves.

Day 144

Dragon:
The truth lies within. I can hold you,
so you can bravely look at it.

Day 145

Cerunos:
Call on me to help with letting go of the
old to make room for the new.

Day 146

Leprechaun:
Do not be afraid to get dirty. Play in the mud. Take a mud bath. Release the toxins and then wash it all off. Have fun while you detox and / or shadow work.

Day 147

Fairy:
It is time to bloom!

Day 148

Gildorf the Gnome:
a shy gnome that works with the plants along the fence line down the laneway and the neighbours yards: It would please us very much and help us too, if folks would consult with us prior to doing yard work, especially the yanking out of plants. Thank you

Day 149

Unicorn:
Are you getting your daily dose of love? If not, call me in to remind you that you are love and therefore able to source yourself.

Day 150

Green Tara:
In nature there is perfection in the chaos.

Day 151

Sprite:
Follow the natural rhythms. Ebb and flow.

Day 152

Goblin:
Your thoughts and emotions can trip you up if you
are not aware of them. Unconscious energies hide
in the shadows. Shine the light on them. Give them
attention. Love them. Respect them as you do the
conscious ones. They are as valuable for they show you
how you can grow. There is truly nothing to fear.

Day 153

Fairy:
Our energy is purer and stronger outside where
nature's energies are. We can work with you indoors
if you ask us to and invite us into your home.
We can help you with your daily living. It would
help us tremendously to have plants about.

Day 154

Dragon:
We are keepers of ancient wisdom. Ancient places and practices are dear to us. When we appear, it means you are ready to connect to the ancient energies.

Day 155

Tree Spirit:
There is no need to do it all alone. We lean on each other, entwine our branches and reach out with our roots to lend a hand. Partnering up is rewarding.

Day 156

Gnome:
call on us to help you stay firmly on the ground. We can even help you walk in difficult footwear or challenging pathways.

Day 157

Fairy Princess of Ottawa- LaOtania:
When walking on nature trails, don't despair if you begin to feel whinny and tired. As an empath you are sensing all the lower energies people who have walked the path before you have left floating around. This is

common for we cannot keep up with the amount of garbage left by the mental and emotional bodies of those that come through. There is nothing wrong with you. Your sensitivity is your gift and you could use it to help us transmute the energies on nature trails.

Day 158

Mermaid:
The State of the oceans and waterways reflect the state of humanity's emotional bodies.

Day 159

Fairy:
Sugar and spice and all that is nice, that is what fairies are made of. Hee-hee. Oh, we do love to play! A little sweet treat is acceptable every once in awhile. Make sure to relish it and celebrate its goodness. From this space, the gratitude you express for it will be truly authentic.

Day 160

Imp:
The reason why you feel tiny and powerless is because you have isolated yourself. Drop your defenses and unite with other like-minded beings.

Day 161

Troll:
I can help you be as fierce or as gentle
as the circumstance requires.

Day 162

Gnome:
The twinkle in the eye comes
from the joy in the heart.

Day 163

Goblin:
I regularly bath in the sun to
cleanse away the shadows.

Day 164

Rock Being:
We weather the elements and still stand strong. We
know that they move energy and help us change.

Day 165

Deva:
Nature is filled with sacred geometry. Sit
with any organic item you find in nature and
contemplate how powerful nature truly is.

Day 166

Fairy:
Be like a dandelion; determined, strong,
resilient. Display your magnificent colour
then with the ease of a gentle breeze, allow
your brilliance to be spread to others.

Day 167

Leprechaun:
Top O' the morning to you. A greeting
is always a respectful action when
interacting with beings in any realm.

Day 168

Pan:
I do not always reveal myself with my manly face. If you
see goat faces, it is I who is trying to gain your attention.

Day 169

Tree Spirit:
Breathe in, breathe out. Flow it in, flow it out.

Day 170

Fairy:
Rest and just be. It is essential to growth.

Day 171

Mermaid:
Your beingness goes deep. Know that you are
safe to explore its vastness. Call on us to help
navigate you through to the jewels you seek.

Day 172

Fairy Queen Maeve:
There is much power in the natural rhythm and cycles.
Honour them and the more you learn to flow with them
the more you will be able to expand with and grace.

Day 173

Unicorn:
Call on us to help you get into play with your permission we can kick away the heavy balls that get in the way. We can show you how to spin a ball to make you light up and sparkle.

Day 174

Dragon:
Call upon us. We are here, every where, waiting for your request.

Day 175

Fairy:
There is so much beauty in the world. When you stop to notice what beauty nature displays at any given moment, you have an opportunity to expand your heart. You can then take that expansion and extend it to the world.

Day 176

Spark:
Light the fires within and keep it stoked by committing time for yourself and pleasures.

Day 177

Rock Being:
We may appear we are sleeping but we
are not. We are actively doing what we
are meant to do. What about you?

Day 178

Gnome:
Call on a crystal gnome to help you
work with the crystals.

Day 179

Phoenix:
Rebirth can be a pleasant experience. Once you
let go of resistance and fear you will see that
burning up and then rising from the ashes can be
enjoyable. Look at it from the result. Getting to
that majestic powerful state is well worth it.

Day 180

Fairy:
Surrender.
Aha! I see you struggling with this word. Let go of
control. You have been holding on so tight for so long

you do not even realize that you are still holding on when you think you let go. Breathe deeply. Breathe deeper. Breathe. Move into your heart and sit there, breathing. Now fill your being with love and joy. Allow these to flow; trusting that whatever you are facing with is perfect for you in this moment. Continue to allow and move through it. Call on us to help you and to bring in ease and grace. Continue to breathe. Now you understand surrender.

Day 181

Tree Spirit:
When you reach for the stars make sure you do so with your feet firmly planted in the earth or you will get lost in space.

Day 182

Goblin:
Don't be afraid of looking into your shadows. That is where the gifts lie.

Day 183

Damara:

Today we in the Elemental Realm, would like you
to consider a few questions. Do you know where
the keys to your heart are? Do you acknowledge
the keys when you get them? Do you keep them
even if you don't know where they fit, or do you
discard them indiscriminately? Do you try to
force the key into a lock that does not fit, or do
you wait patiently for the right lock to appear?

Prayer of Gratitude to the Elements
Sprites, thank you for sending the rain to
cleanse, nourish and hydrate nature
Sparks, thank you for the sun's rays for
lighting the world and providing warmth
Terra, thank you for the firmness on which we can
stand and the fertility in which to grow our food
Sylphs, thank you for sustaining us with
the fresh air that we breathe

Day 184

Fairy Queen Maeve:
Out in nature, you will often come across elemental
sentinel who will spot you and decide whether they
will reveal themselves to you. They also notify
all of the other beings in the area of your arrival.
If you have gained their trust you may be blessed
with an appearance of an elemental being such as a
fairy or a gnome. If your heart is pure and of noble
intention you may even be led to a fairy court.

Day 185

Leprechaun:
Many have attributed hope to the symbol of the
rainbow. We suggest that you drop hope for it sets up
expectations and leads to disappointment. Perhaps

you can associate trust with rainbows for it is more likely to open the doors to the infinite possibilities.

Day 186

Sprite:
What is your reflection saying?

Day 187

Tree Spirit:
You may sometimes feel like you are pulled in 2 opposing directions but if you are solidly grounded, you can handle it.

Day 188

Fairy:
Adventure comes in many forms and you can embrace it in many ways.

Day 189

Gnome:
Connect to the earth and you will be supported.

Day 190

Sylph:
When it rains, we dance in the water droplets and wash away the old debris and refill all with joy and love.

Day 191

Tree Elf:
Know that you are protected. All you have to do is ask for we honour your free will. Once you ask, we can quickly and happily step in.

Day 192

Fairy:
Listen to the music that nature's orchestra plays.

Day 193

Imp:
Many insects, arachnids and even mollusks make silk to weave webs, build nests, to bond to rocks or to cocoon in. Some are created to capture nourishment, some as safety lines, others to create a home or create a pod for transformation and rebirth. This is their gift for their mission work. If you are seeing webs or

cocoons in your environment, then we are drawing your attention to how you could be using your gifts.

Day 194

Wizard:
Time is an illusion. It is a spell cast to constrict you. Be aware of the game it plays. The more you play with it, the more constricted you will feel.

Day 195

Rock Being:
Our wisdom runs deep. We can guide you to the vein of true richness.

Day 196

Spark:
Find your circle of illumination.

Day 197

Dragon:
Trust the process. If you are truly doing the inner work, know that you will arrive where you need to when you need to. Resistance, rushing, pushing,

comparing and complaining only succeeds in slowing the process down. Yet, it is brilliant as well because you have an opportunity to learn and grow in each of these states. Know that each being has their own path and list of lessons to learn as well as their own list of items to transmute. Many old souls have chosen to return and clear much from all their previous lives and this takes time.

Day 198

Elf:
We are master teachers and if you are a willing student you can learn some amazing subjects.

Day 199

Fairy:
You are limited only by your imagination.

Day 200

St. Francis:
The melodies offered by the birds are coded songs played to all the beings in the area. It is up to each to receive them.

Day 201

Sprite:
The waves are the best place to play.

Day 202

Elf:
Serenade yourself.

Day 203

Gnome:
When you are in nature, be in the stillness for
a bit and allow the energies to flow through
your feet to clear out the gunk. Only then can
you receive the goodness nature offers.

Day 204

Deva:
After planning, structuring, preparing, working
and nurturing your intentions, take a moment
to see what has resulted. Enjoy the success.

Day 205

Mermaid:
Allow your imagination to flow.

Day 206

Fairy:
Live, Love, Sparkle

Day 207

Sprite:
Hydrate your body and hydrate your soul.

Day 208

Dragon:
We look fearsome in order to get your attention,
so you can look at the lies you tell yourself.

Day 209

Fairy:
Beauty can be found in the simplest things.

Day 210

Mermaid:
Many humans have a fascination with seashells. This is because they recognize that it is a link to their true essence and a link to a time long forgotten. It is a call to dive deep into your soul and into the oneness of the universe, so you can tap into the sacred energies.

Day 211

Tree Spirit:
Get comfortable with the chaos. There is perfection in the chaos for it creates upheaval in order to clear the old and allow space for the new.

Day 212

Fairy Queen Maeve:
Power of Play: "You can not be in joy, flow, love or play if you are out of alignment. When you are in alignment, these are natural. If you are flowing, the higher vibrations will flow.

Day 213

Unicorn:
Call upon us to help clear your chakras. We
will come charging in to do so. You will then be
able to bring in higher vibrational energies.

Day 214

Cerunos:
Live in the moment. That is where all
the creative and sourcing energy is.

Day 215

Deva:
Most animals have a tail, whether it be short, long,
scaly or fluffy. The tail is there to help them to balance
as they move through their environment. In your
evolution in walking upright, the balance is achieved
in the legs and feet, so the tail is no longer required.
You have lost your tail, yet you have not lost your tail
bone and that is to remind you to always find your
balance as you move through your environment.

Day 216

Terra:
Roots go deep in search of nutrients where the soil is rich and fertile. Send your roots down deep in order to nourish yourself.

Day 217

Unicorn:
There is an infinite number of ways of being. Which resonates most with your inner truth?

Day 218

Fairy:
Scintillating is a word you can include in your daily life.

Day 219

Spark:
Nourish yourself in the flames of passion;
passion for your work, sexual passion,
creative passion, all your passions.

Day 220

Goblin:
You receive snippets of information. Therefore, your
perspective is skewed towards the snippet you hold.

Day 221

Rock Being:
Often the ancient secrets are locked within us for
safe keeping until such time it is safe to release the
knowledge. I can help you unlock secrets within yourself
if you are willing to face the challenges to get to them.

Day 222

Archangel Ariel:
The trees love you, the rocks love you, the
elementals loves you, natures loves you,
Source loves you and I love you.

Day 223

Sprite:
Stop by a river, creek or even a fountain and play
with us. We love to play and it would be a privilege to
play with you. Just call us and we will come forth.

Day 224

Fairy:
Fill yourself up with joy and love. Pack it in tight until
it bursts out of you. Now share it with everyone you
meet. It will put sparkles in your step and theirs as well.

Day 225

Tree Spirit:
Face the dark as there is always light behind it.

Day 226

Sylph:
Your thoughts and feelings ripple out in
concentric circles. Like a stone tossed in the
water, the energy flows everywhere. You have
the power to choose what ripples out.

Day 227

Unicorn:
We are master healers. Invite us to work on you.
Allow us to do our work. Then follow our guidance.
The first prompting you have is us guiding you to
the best physical support to anchor the healing.

Day 228

Aine:
In the expression of the truest form of love, animal
companions have been taking on the pain of the
lessons, so their people do not have to feel it. It is
time to take responsibility for your own lessons.

Day 229

Gnome:
It is wise when harvesting the fruits of your labour to reinvest more of what you love for the next season.

Day 230

Phoenix:
You will know of my presence when you feel a wave of heat move through you and then notice a significant change in your state.

Day 231

Dragon:
When you have played with a dragon, give it a big hug of gratitude! We just love hugs.

Day 232

Fairy:
Find your individual songs and share them!

Day 233

Wizard:
Squashing energies to get rid of them could result in messy outcomes. Transmute the energies. That's the cleanest and easiest way to change the situation.

Day 234

Gaia:
I am your home. Know that while you are embodied here you are home. Sink your roots further into me and feel the comfort.

Day 235

Cerunos:
As the seasons shift, stagnation slows down in winter's freezing only to regain speed again in the spring in order to source the new growth. If you are freezing stagnation in yourself to avoid the decay you will find it a challenge to deal with when it does thaw. If you allow the stagnation to flow at its natural pace you find it nourishing in the spring.

Day 236

Troll:
I am as shy as you yet if I have come to help
you, it is more efficient to hold my gaze. I can
then truly mirror what needs to move. With a
bang, we shall move the energy together.

Day 237

Fairy:
Fragrant flower scents is one of our specialities. Use
floral waters or essential oils to enhance your specialties.

Day 238

Sprite:
Stagnation has a purpose in nature. It is where plant
material decays. Call on us to help you move the
emotions, so they don't stagnate in your body.

Day 239

Rock Being:
Do not be fooled by our appearance. We are as alive
as you are. We may not move physically unless due
an external force, but we travel interdimensionally.
You may find it ironic that we are some of the

densest matter on the planet and yet we can shift so easily. We look forward to being your teachers.

Day 240

Unicorn:
Anytime you are doing work from the heart, call on us and we can assist, guide, protect, enhance and support you.

Day 241

Aine:
When you garden, or farm be in the sacred awareness of the life-giving qualities. Be present with it from the seed to the cultivated food and back to the seed collection. Every moment in that cycle is precious and should be nurtured. The same holds true if you raise animals. If you do not garden or farm, then be in sacred awareness when you shop and prepare your food. Honour your food.

Day 242

St Francis:
Keep it simple. Although the universal energies and the Elemental Realm are complex, connecting and working with the beings as well as all earth's creatures is quite simple.

Day 243

Dragon:
You cannot rush a dragon. We will tell you
when we are ready to work. Be patient.

Day 244

Fairy:
Life is an adventure. Walk the path being
open to discover its wonders.

Day 245

Sylph:
Don't just let your worries float in the wind currents
for us to clean up. Instead, use the wind currents to
consciously process them and to bring in the clean air.

Day 246

Unicorn:
There is a long held belief that we are loners. This is
an untruth. We live in herds. We are a community,
and everyone is part of our tribe. We also work with
and seek counsels with other tribes. We see this
same loner false belief in many of you. There is no
need to do everything on your own or to walk your
path alone. It is time to reconnect to your tribe.

Day 247

Pan:
Tap into the creative energies of fertility. This can
be accessed at anytime of the year. Even when
nature sleeps, she is fertile in many ways.

Day 248

Fairy Princess of Ottawa- LaOtania:
Get to know the fairies and fairy courts in your
local area. They are powerful allies to work with.

Day 249

Mermaid:
Splish, splash! Take some time out of your
busy schedules to have some fun. Let your
hair down and let loose. Feel into the rhythms
and break out your dance moves.

Day 250

Goblin:
Your addictions just may come from the separation
from Gaia and the elemental realm. Get outside
and connect to the magical blissful energies of
nature and marvel at the beauty and wonder.

Day 251

Damara:
There are some in the Elemental Realm who have
lost their way. The darkness holds them and guides
them. We ask for your assistance in holding the
light of love in your heart for them and then do
no more. They must learn their lessons just as you
must learn yours. Just as it is your responsibility
to take that first step and ask for help in seeking
the light, it is their responsibility to do so.

Day 252

Dragon:
Stand tall and be proud. You have accomplished much.
It takes a lot of courage to shine your light bright.
You have it in you and I know you have what it takes
to be the bright shinning light that you came to be.

Day 253

Troll:
Trust me to help you to move into
that place of inner glow.

Day 254

Unicorn:
Self mastery means being aware of the energy flow.

Day 255

Spark:
Sore, hot and inflamed parts of your body are areas
of stagnant energy. It is us trying to draw your
attention to the area. Focus your attention on it and
use the heat to burn the old trapped gunk. Call on
us to amplify the clearing and to guide you to the
appropriate actions to heal the physical body.

Day 256

4 Elements:
Working with us individually is powerful. Working
with us in a combination or even better with all
4 of us is even more powerful. Look at how a
tornado functions. The water and the heat in the
air moves into the dry cool air and with strong
winds creates a spin and pulls up the earth.

Day 257

Leprechaun:
Even the young leprechauns are old by your
standards. But we young ones have more fun than
the wiser of our kind! The more humanity expands
and believes in us, many younger leprechauns will
come forth. We are excited to work with you.

Day 258

Aine:
Call on me to help soothe your animal companion.

Day 259

Fairy:
Believe in all possibilities

Day 260

Mermaid:
It is more important to acknowledge and see what is under the surface than to float at the surface. Call on me to take you to new depths of exploration.

Day 261

Elf:
We are master artisans of ancient crafts. We have taught many humans in the past and look forward to resuming our teachings.

Day 262

Gnome:
The grass is not greener on the other side of the fence. It only looks that way because you see the light shinning into it. Others are looking back and seeing the light shine through your grass thinking it is greener on your side. If you are going to jump over the fence, jump for a different reason than the greener grass.

Day 263

Deva:
Your body is your vehicle. Here are
some questions to ask yourself.
Are you driving a jalopy or a high-end vehicle?
Do you invest in regular maintenance or
do you just keep pushing through?
What is the quality of the fuel you
use to run your vehicle?
What do you do to prepare your
vehicle for the season's change?
Are you consistent with all of this?
Where do you want your vehicle to go?
You hold the power to ensure that your vehicle
gets you to your destination. If you struggle
with any aspect related to your vehicle, seek
help. Ask me to help guide you to the highest
and best solution for you in the moment.

Day 264

Damara:
Your children and even your inner child deserves the
purest most authentic love to be showered on them.

Day 265

Fairy:
Enjoy the fairy energy when you encounter it
but be careful when you come across a fairy
kingdom. If you are not used to or vibrating high
enough to handle the energies, you could become
addicted to the bliss and not want to leave.

Day 266

Wizard:
Spells are very powerful and should be
used wisely. Every vow you make is a
spell that is binding in that wish.

Day 267

Goblin:
The beauty is everywhere. It is how you look at it.

Day 268

Dragon:
call upon us to burn through blocks so that you
can see the truth. We will do so with love.

Day 269

Sylph:
Dance in the rain and celebrate the joyous event.

Day 270

Aine:
All of the animals and plants on the planet
hold qualities and codes that are needed for the
functioning of the environment that they live in.
These are shared with you in the water you drink,
the air you breathe and the food you eat. As air
and water circulate the planet, these qualities also
circulate. If a species goes extinct naturally, then
the service they provided is no longer needed. If
a species goes extinct due to human intervention,
then you loose necessary qualities and codes.

Day 271

Unicorn:
One of our specialties is to transmute poisons.
Call on us to help transmute poisons within
you so that you can easily move forward.

Day 272

Fairy:
Love what you do. If you are feeling stuck in work
or performing tasks that you do not love doing
find ways to love portions of it. Find ways to love
the daily chores. Find activities that you love
doing. Slowly increase what you love doing.

Day 273

Leprechaun:
Know when to be serious and when to play.
It is an important aspect of balance. Call
on me if you need assistance with this.

<u>Wizard Potion Recipe</u>
Goblin: Reveal the shadows
Spark: Transmute the shadows
Leprechaun: Shower with rainbow light
Fairy: Sparkle your life with fun and play

Day 274

St. Francis:
Take a walk outside and take a moment to smell
the flowers. You will be so much happier for it.

Day 275

Goblin:
I appear ugly because the truth lies in the
ugliness. Are you brave enough to look at it?

Day 276

Troll:
Anger can cloud the judgment. Use your feet to
move it. Stomp it out and allow Gaia to take it.
Allow her to replace it with love and clarity.

Day 277

Elf:
Focus on your breathing

Day 278

Rock Being:
Appearances can be deceiving. What appears
inert and lifeless can be full of life. Be sure
to check before jumping to conclusions.

Day 279

Deva:
In nature is where the magic happens.
Guess what? You are part of nature.

Day 280

Spark:
It is time to burn the old to make way for the new.

Day 281

Wizard:
Alchemy involves transmuting lead into gold.
What does that mean to you? What is the
lead in your life? What is the gold in your life?
You can transmute anything into anything.
Note that the process goes both ways.

Day 282

Fairy Queen Maeve:
Your clairs are doorways. Which doorway do
you leave open to welcome elementals in?

Day 283

Unicorn:
Whether I appear to you as masculine or feminine,
I hold both energies in balance. Call on me to align
your masculine and feminine so they are in balance.

Day 284

Fairy:
Connect to your inner child and make life an adventure.

Day 285

Tree Spirit:
Growth occurs in layers. Instant growth all at once
would result in fragile tissues and the being would not
be able to sustain the weight and movement of life.

Day 286

Leprechaun:
Break out your silliness. It is important to nourish the
playful and whimsical side. There is no need to put
pressure on yourself. You do not need to be the life of
the party. You can be silly in your personal space.

Day 287

Sprite & Sylph:
Flush your body everyday with water. Follow it with
conscious breathing to get the oxygen flowing.

Day 288

Dragon:
We are equipped to deal with whatever comes at us
in order to transmute the lower vibrations so that
you can allow in love and light in order to be able
to see the truth. The reason why we have scales is
to be able to withstand the attack when someone is
unable to look within and deal with the truth that
they are facing. The reason why we have horns, sharp
claws and big teeth is to stab, butt, rip, shred and
tear into the lower vibrational energies projected at
us. The reason why we breathe fire is to transmute
the lower vibrations you release. The reason why
we have wings is to sweep away the lower energies
that are around you and to provide protection when
needed. We are equipped to deal with your fear,
anger or grief. We are powerful enough to hold the
space needed for you to see the truth and transmute
anything in the way of reaching that truth.

Day 289

Gnome:
We can help you excavate the debris within
in. Call on us when working on clearing.

Day 290

Fairy:
Go outside and marvel at the wondrous colours and
soak in the majestic beauty. It is the best therapy of all!

Day 291

Cerunos:
Pay attention to how you respond to the natural
cycles especially with the season changes and
how the length of daylight affects you.

Day 292

Rock Being:
Rocks that have quartz in them, glisten in the sun.
We sparkle for you. When this catches your attention,
come sit on the rock or pick us up. We want to get
to know your amazing brilliance and share ours.

Day 293

Fairy:
Enjoy life.

Day 294

The 4 Elements:
All of the elements have sparkle factor. Crystal pieces sparkle in the sunlight. Fire shoots up sparkles in the sky. Water and snow create sparkly diamonds in the sunlight. Air sparkles with static electricity. Sparkles mirror beauty and ignite joy. Sparkling is a fundamental necessity to life. What sparkles are you creating in your life that can be enjoyed by those around you?

Day 295

Green Man:
In the fall the deciduous trees pull the nutrients to the core and down to the roots to prepare for the journey within. As a result, the leaves are no longer fed, and they drop away. This process of letting go protects the tree during the harsh winter weather. This is a very important part of the process that allows the trees to incubate the new growth over winter.

Day 296

Mermaid:
Reach out of your element every once in
a while, to gain a fresh perspective.

Day 297

Unicorn:
Get to know the healing side of the shadow side.

Day 298

Dragon:
In legends of old, dragons were said to be keepers,
lol, even hoarders, of gold, jewels and gems. The
truth is we are the protectors of the Divine Truth

and all that is linked to it. We are happy to share
these treasures to anyone willing to face the truth.

Day 299

Fairy:
Care for yourself. There is no need to put pressure on
yourself. You are on a journey, a grand adventure. Go
with the flow of your journey. Enjoy your adventure.

Day 300

Fire & Air:
How are you blocking the sun in your life? Believe
that the power is always there even with obstacles.

Day 301

Unicorn:
Look for the beauty is within.

Day 302

Fairy:
The light comes from within; shine it.

Day 303

Sylph:
How are you suddenly freezing up your emotions? The air element is activated to assist in blowing away emotional energies you are ready to thaw and let go of now.

Day 304

Spark:
It is time to burn away the old. Take time to look ahead and see what will support you best.

Day 305

Green Tara:
Use your internal fires to light your way.

Day 306

Aine:
I can help bridge the communication between you and your animal companion. I can see the blocks in both of you and work around them. If you are ready to clear the blocks, I can help with that as well.

Day 307

Troll:
Working together means believing. Believing
in us and believing in yourself.

Day 308

Fairy:
Everyone has a unique vibrational signature. Your gifts
align to the vibration. When you speak from the heart,
that vibration is shared. Go out and sing your song.

Day 309

Dragon:
It is wisest to take bite size chunks out of any
challenges, so you do not choke yourself. Take your
time and chew before moving to the next bite.

Day 310

Terra:
If you are finding it difficult to stay
grounded, call on me for assistance.

Day 311

St. Francis:
Change can provoke fear which can bring about unnecessary challenges. Know that change is a constant natural process in life. Expect it. Welcome it. Call on any of your wise councils to help you.

Day 312

Deva:
Flap your wings and fly with the fairies.

Day 313

Wizard:
You have the power to cast spells. Believe in the power of words. Whether spoken out loud or internally, the spell is cast.

Day 314

Fairy:
Expanding your heart with gratitude, love and joy is the key to getting into the Elemental Realm.

Day 315

Unicorn:
Challenges will occur in life. They are to be expected for without them you cannot grow. Without growth, your incarnation is without purpose. Yet it does not mean that you must overcome them all on your own. I am here to assist you in any way that I can and specially to help you see the challenge from the point of view of the heart.

Day 316

Dragon:
We are often guided to redirect souls who move away from their path. Pay attention to our signs. We work with each individual differently, so it is important to build a relationship with us. Together we can develop a plan for ease and grace.

Day 317

Spark:
Go ahead and heat up your life with your passion.

Day 318

Goblin:
We reveal the good, the bad and the ugly. Yet it is all beautiful because it is all truth. Once you shine the light of truth on the ugly bits the beauty shines through.

Day 319

Imp:
Look at how the dragonflies glitter in the light. Dragonfly and I can teach you how to dazzle up your being.

Day 320

Pan:
I play the pipes for soothing and to bring enjoyment. The sylphs love to dance through the pipes and share melodious vibrations. Regularly we play our music in nature making sounds through tubular material to soothe your soul and remind you to take time to enjoy the little wonders of the world.

Day 321

Unicorn:
Gifting is an important aspect to balancing
receiving. Make sure to gift to yourself.

Day 322

Sylph:
Breath in the freshness in the air.

Day 323

St. Francis:
The nature spirits remind always that we are loved.
Sometimes it is not evident and sometimes we
are not able to see past our pain in the moment,
but we are loved every second. They leave us
reminders that our purpose is to be love.

Day 324

Fairy:
We love it when you have fun and play. We want
to play with you. Call us in for the fun!

Day 325

Unicorn:
Imagination opens the door to the possibilities.

Day 326

Wizard:
♫ Magic, there is magic, everywhere
you look there is magic. ♫

Day 327

Dragon:
We are more than happy to serve as a symbol
of something to vanquish just as long as once
the dragon dies, you acknowledge that within
yourself and vanquish it as well. We would like
you to be your own hero. However, it is much
more powerful and magical to work with us to
transmute that part of you that no longer serves.

Day 328

Fairy:
When you are buzzing along in life, remember to
stop for a minute to enjoy your surroundings.

Day 329

Wizard:
Cast magical spells of beauty with
loving words and actions.

Day 330

Fairy Princess of Ottawa- LaOtania:
Continue to delight in the magic of nature
and we will continue to delight you with our

offerings. We love it so when you notice and
appreciate the beauty nature displays.

Day 331

Snow Fairy:
Every snowflake is a handcrafted crystal delivering
unique qualities for nature to receive. Like all crystals,
they are amplifiers and can be programmed. When you
project your negativity when it snows you are clearing
the qualities nature needs and reprogramming the snow
crystals with lower vibrations for nature to receive. The
crystals are designed so that joy amplifies the qualities
imbued in them. All we ask though is that you be in
gratitude for the snow and for the work it performs.

Day 332

The 4 elements:
Your body may consist primarily of water, but
you still require a balance of all the elements
moving through you to remain healthy.

Day 333

Gaia:
As a living being, I must detoxify regularly. I am
home to many different beings and process all of their

toxins. This equals a tremendous amount of powerful energy that must move out of my body. I invite you to work with me in the detoxification process. You can do this in a variety of ways yet primarily in being responsible for toxins coming from your bodies.

Day 334

Fairy:
Be love.

Day 335

Spark:
The warmth is where the heart is.

Day 336

Elf:
Promote good will.

Day 337

Leprechaun:
I hold the secrets of the rainbow, but it is not the pot of gold that you believe it to be.

Day 338

Troll:
Getting caught up in the drama constricts
the heart chakra and blocks the flow.

Day 339

Fairy:
We are a community. An individual does not do
everything on their own. The work is shared and
no one being claims ownership or status. Everyone
takes pride in their work and view it as contribution
to the greater whole. The more we invest in our
work and with joy the greater the outcome will
be for the whole. We are collaborative beings.

Day 340

Gnome:
Humanity has a great need for labeling. We understand
your mind's need to comprehend and sort matter.
However, there is a line where the labeling constricts the
energy and prevents the energy from freely attaining its
true form. Not everything requires a name or a word.
Rather, feel into the energy and you will know its truth.

Day 341

Dragon:
We have scales for protection. Ensuring
that you have proper protection is essential.
We are equipped to protect you.

Day 342

Ice Fairy:
Don't rush the process or be in a hurry to get
to somewhere. It's like driving on ice. The
faster you go, the more risk of sliding into the
ditch. If you do find yourself sliding, the more
you try to control the steering the more you
spin and slide. Slow down and let go of control
and allow the universal flow to guide you.

Day 343

Tree Spirit on Dewberry Trail:
Be real. No matter the circumstances be authentic.

Day 344

Goblin:
When you feel like there is nothing but darkness
around you, celebrate! It means that you are in a place

of great growth potential. We need the shadows. Without them, you could not see the light. I am built to inhabit the dark. Walk with me and I will guide you through the shadows, so you find the light.

Day 345

Terra:
We are in nearly everything on the planet. We are in the earth, the plants, the trees, the animals, you, rocks and even the river bed. We are matter. Everything we are a part of matters.

Day 346

Damara:
All the beings in the Elemental Realm are my children. I ask your assistance in caring for them.

Day 347

Sprite:
Dance in the rain and celebrate the joyous event.

Day 348

Leprechaun:
Believe.

Day 349

Rock Being:
Each crystal, each rock, has its own unique
wisdom to share based on the material
elements composed in that crystal or rock.

Day 350

Winter Deva:
Call upon the ice and frost elementals to keep your skin
safe when out in the cold. We would be delighted to
help if your higher self is willing. Please note that this is
a temporary fix and not to prolong your stay in the cold.

Day 351

Wizard:
A wizard spends many years, sometimes even
lifetimes, learning and perfecting his craft. That is
because the manipulation of energies has an infinite
number of possible outcomes with the potential for
greatness in any direction. Patience and practice

in understanding how the energies move and the possible outcomes are essential to mastery.

Day 352

Troll:
I can help shine the light on where the boundaries need to be set. I can also help you set and maintain proper boundaries.

Day 353

Tree Spirit:
Wisdom is shared truth. Truth is revealed in many forms. Open up your entire being to receive truth in any form.

Day 354

Fairy:
Be good to yourself.

Day 355

Cerunos:
Know that there is light at the end of the tunnel. First you must be willing to travel the tunnel.

Day 356

Gnome:
Travel to your heart. Sit there for a while
and breathe. Listen to the stillness.

Day 357

Snow Fairy:
Blanket yourself in quiet time and
allow yourself to rejuvenate.

Day 358

Goblin:
Now that you have mastered finding me in the
shadows, look for me in the light. Once you
are comfortable looking at your ugly side, I can
show you how to use the light to transform it.

Day 359

Tree Spirit:
When you feel like you are confused and lost, don't
get your roots in a knot. Send them deep down to be
sourced and bring up the knowledge you are seeking.

Day 360

Damara:
The Elemental Realm is a vast and complicated
world. Many beings would like you to know
that we are happy collaborators and look
forward to reuniting in our work.

Day 361

Snow Elf:
There is so much unique majestic beauty and
wisdom in every snowflake. You are a snowflake.

Day 362

Phoenix:
You will know of my presence when you feel
a wave of heat move through you and then
notice a significant change in your state.

Day 363

Rock Being:
A solid foundation of trust is required
to withstand the weather.

Day 364

Unicorn:
Call on us to help you to laser in
on and sharpen your focus.

Day 365

Leprechaun:
Celebrate! Have some fun but to know
what kind of shenanigans to get into.

Leap Year Day

Fairy:
If you are consistent and do the work, you will
find that you will progress in leaps and bounds.

A Closing Word

Thank you for taking this journey with the Elementals Realm beings. I hope you enjoyed their messages and were able to find comfort and guidance in them.

Here is a parting message from the
Celtic Earth Goddess Aeracura:

Remember to just quietly be. Like a flower. The
bees and the butterflies that come by and leave;
they are attracted to your beauty and gifts. This
is your purpose to share these and just be.

When you bloom, your purpose is to display your
beauty and your gifts. During this time, enjoy the sun,
the rain, the wind and the nature visitors. When this
purpose is done, you bloom another beauty and gift to
share. Like all flowers there is the time of unfolding.

A flower does not bloom 24/7. When it
is spent, honour it and let it go, trusting
that a new bloom will take its place.

Printed in the United States
By Bookmasters